TRUMPET
101 CHRISTMAS SONGS

Available for
FLUTE, CLARINET, ALTO SAX, TENOR SAX, TRUMPET,
HORN, TROMBONE, VIOLIN, VIOLA, CELLO

ISBN 978-1-5400-3024-5

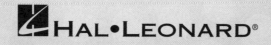

Visit Hal Leonard Online at
www.halleonard.com

Contact Us:
Hal Leonard
7777 West Bluemound Road
Milwaukee, WI 53213
Email: info@halleonard.com

In Europe contact:
Hal Leonard Europe Limited
42 Wigmore Street
Marylebone, London, W1U 2RN
Email: info@halleonardeurope.com

In Australia contact:
Hal Leonard Australia Pty. Ltd.
4 Lentara Court
Cheltenham, Victoria, 3192 Australia
Email: info@halleonard.com.au

CONTENTS

4   All I Want for Christmas Is You

5   Angels from the Realms of Glory

8   Angels We Have Heard on High

6   As Long as There's Christmas

8   Auld Lang Syne

9   Away in a Manger (Murray)

12   Away in a Manger (Spilman)

10   Baby, It's Cold Outside

12   Because It's Christmas (For All the Children)

14   Believe

19   The Bells of St. Mary's

15   Blue Christmas

16   Brazilian Sleigh Bells

18   Caroling, Caroling

20   A Child Is Born

20   The Chipmunk Song

22   Christmas (Baby Please Come Home)

21   Christmas in Killarney

23   Christmas Is A-Comin' (May God Bless You)

24   The Christmas Song (Chestnuts Roasting on an Open Fire)

28   Christmas Time Is Here

28   The Christmas Waltz

26   Cold December Night

29   Dance of the Sugar Plum Fairy

30   Deck the Hall

30   Do You Hear What I Hear

25   Do You Want to Build a Snowman?

32   Fairytale of New York

34   Feliz Navidad

31   The First Noel

33   God Rest Ye Merry, Gentlemen

37   Good King Wenceslas

35   Grandma Got Run Over by a Reindeer

36   The Greatest Gift of All

38   Grown-Up Christmas List

42   Happy Holiday

40   Happy Xmas (War Is Over)

42   Hard Candy Christmas

39   Hark! The Herald Angels Sing

41   Have Yourself a Merry Little Christmas

43   Here Comes Santa Claus (Right Down Santa Claus Lane)

45   A Holly Jolly Christmas

44   (There's No Place Like) Home for the Holidays

45   I Heard the Bells on Christmas Day (Calkin)

48   I Heard the Bells on Christmas Day (Marks)

48   I Saw Mommy Kissing Santa Claus

49   I Saw Three Ships

46   I Want a Hippopotamus for Christmas (Hippo the Hero)

49   I Wonder as I Wander

47 I'll Be Home for Christmas

50 I've Got My Love to Keep Me Warm

53 It Came Upon the Midnight Clear

52 It Must Have Been the Mistletoe (Our First Christmas)

51 It's Beginning to Look Like Christmas

54 Jingle Bells

56 Joy to the World

54 The Last Month of the Year (What Month Was Jesus Born In?)

55 Let It Snow! Let It Snow! Let It Snow!

57 Little Saint Nick

58 March of the Toys

59 A Marshmallow World

60 Mary, Did You Know?

56 Mary's Little Boy Child

64 Mele Kalikimaka

61 Merry Christmas, Darling

64 Mister Santa

65 Mistletoe and Holly

62 The Most Wonderful Time of the Year

63 My Favorite Things

68 O Christmas Tree

68 O Come, All Ye Faithful

66 O Holy Night

66 O Little Town of Bethlehem

69 Parade of the Wooden Soldiers

70 Pretty Paper

71 Rockin' Around the Christmas Tree

72 Rudolph the Red-Nosed Reindeer

73 Santa Baby

67 Santa Claus Is Comin' to Town

74 Shake Me I Rattle (Squeeze Me I Cry)

78 Silent Night

74 Silver and Gold

75 Silver Bells

78 Sing We Now of Christmas

79 Somewhere in My Memory

79 The Star Carol

76 That's Christmas to Me

80 This Christmas

81 Toyland

83 The Twelve Days of Christmas

81 Up on the Housetop

82 We Need a Little Christmas

86 We Three Kings of Orient Are

86 We Wish You a Merry Christmas

84 We Wish You the Merriest

87 What Are You Doing New Year's Eve?

90 What Child Is This?

90 White Christmas

88 Wonderful Christmastime

92 The Wonderful World of Christmas

91 You're All I Want for Christmas

ALL I WANT FOR CHRISTMAS IS YOU

TRUMPET

Words and Music by MARIAH CAREY
and WALTER AFANASIEFF

Moderately fast

(small notes optional)

ANGELS FROM THE REALMS OF GLORY

Words by JAMES MONTGOMERY
Music by HENRY T. SMART

AS LONG AS THERE'S CHRISTMAS

from BEAUTY AND THE BEAST - THE ENCHANTED CHRISTMAS

TRUMPET

Music by RACHEL PORTMAN
Lyrics by DON BLACK

Moderately

AULD LANG SYNE

Words by ROBERT BURNS
Traditional Scottish Melody

Moderately

ANGELS WE HAVE HEARD ON HIGH

Traditional French Carol

Moderately

AWAY IN A MANGER

Music by JAMES R. MURRAY

BABY, IT'S COLD OUTSIDE

TRUMPET

By FRANK LOESSER

Moderately

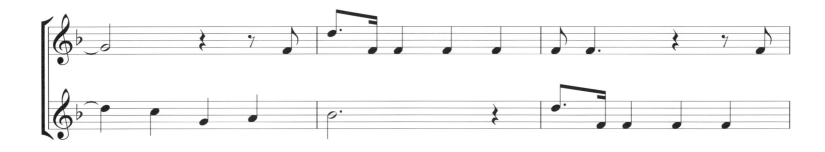

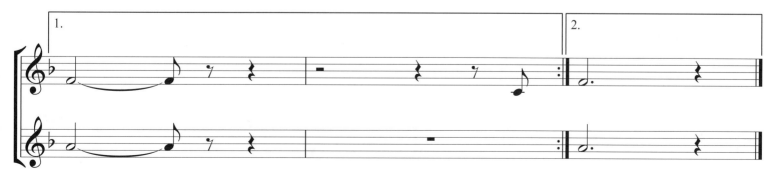

AWAY IN A MANGER

TRUMPET

Music by JONATHAN E. SPILMAN

Sweetly

BECAUSE IT'S CHRISTMAS

(For All the Children)

Music by BARRY MANILOW
Lyric by BRUCE SUSSMAN and JACK FELDMAN

Moderately slow

BELIEVE
from Warner Bros. Pictures' THE POLAR EXPRESS

TRUMPET

Words and Music by GLEN BALLARD
and ALAN SILVESTRI

Moderately slow

BLUE CHRISTMAS

Words and Music by BILLY HAYES
and JAY JOHNSON

With expression

BRAZILIAN SLEIGH BELLS

TRUMPET

By PERCY FAITH

Bright Samba

To Coda

TRUMPET

CAROLING, CAROLING

Words by WIHLA HUTSON
Music by ALFRED BURT

THE BELLS OF ST. MARY'S

TRUMPET

Traditional
Words by DOUGLAS FURBER
Music by A. EMMETT ADAMS

Slowly, with freedom

A CHILD IS BORN

By THAD JONES

THE CHIPMUNK SONG

Words and Music by
ROSS BAGDASARIAN

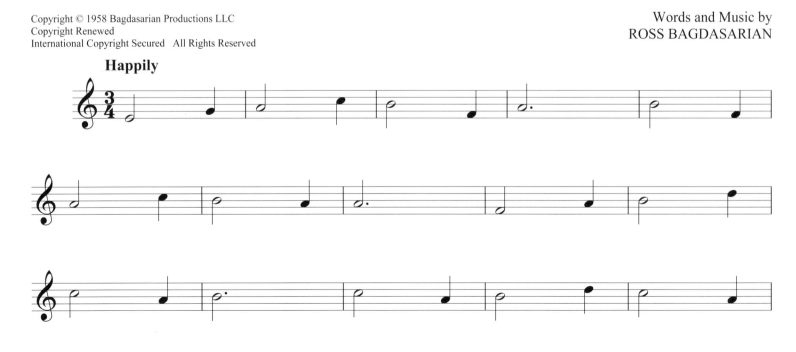

CHRISTMAS IN KILLARNEY

Words and Music by JOHN REDMOND
and FRANK WELDON

Moderately, with a lilt

CHRISTMAS
(Baby Please Come Home)

TRUMPET

Words and Music by PHIL SPECTOR,
ELLIE GREENWICH and JEFF BARRY

CHRISTMAS IS A-COMIN'
(May God Bless You)

TRUMPET

Words and Music by
FRANK LUTHER

Moderately slow

1., 2.

3. **Very slowly**

THE CHRISTMAS SONG
(Chestnuts Roasting on an Open Fire)

TRUMPET

Music and Lyric by MEL TORMÉ
and ROBERT WELLS

Moderately

DO YOU WANT TO BUILD A SNOWMAN?

from FROZEN

TRUMPET

Music and Lyrics by KRISTEN ANDERSON-LOPEZ
and ROBERT LOPEZ

COLD DECEMBER NIGHT

TRUMPET

Words and Music by MICHAEL BUBLE,
ALAN CHANG and ROBERT ROCK

CHRISTMAS TIME IS HERE
from A CHARLIE BROWN CHRISTMAS

Words by LEE MENDELSON
Music by VINCE GUARALDI

Slowly

THE CHRISTMAS WALTZ

Words by SAMMY CAHN
Music by JULE STYNE

Moderately, with expression

DANCE OF THE SUGAR PLUM FAIRY
from THE NUTCRACKER

By PYOTR IL'YICH TCHAIKOVSKY

Quickly

(small notes optional)

DECK THE HALL

Traditional Welsh Carol

Brightly

DO YOU HEAR WHAT I HEAR

Words and Music by NOEL REGNEY
and GLORIA SHAYNE

Moderately

To Coda

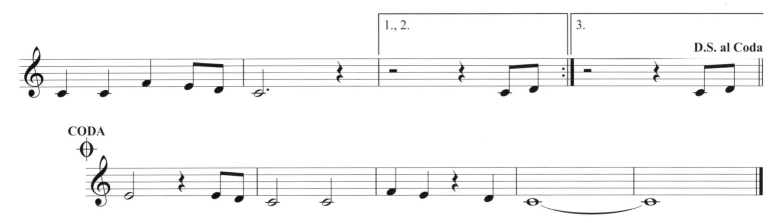

THE FIRST NOEL

17th Century English Carol
Music from W. Sandys' *Christmas Carols*

FAIRYTALE OF NEW YORK

TRUMPET

Words and Music by JEREMY FINER
and SHANE MacGOWAN

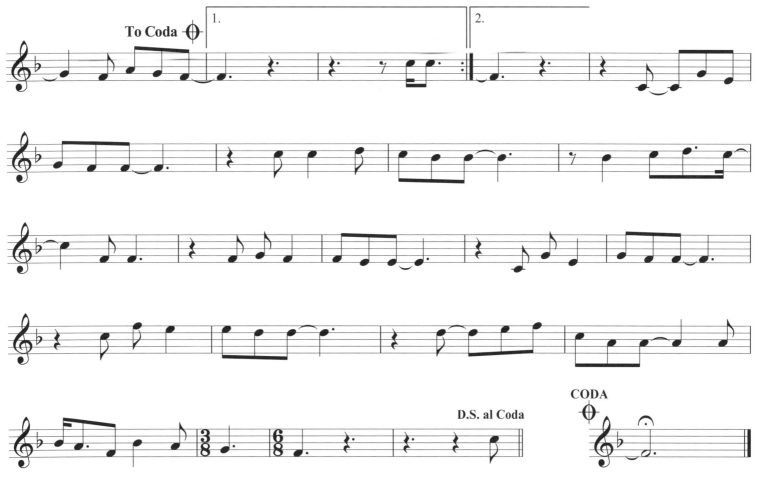

GOD REST YE MERRY, GENTLEMEN

Traditional English Carol

FELIZ NAVIDAD

TRUMPET

Music and Lyrics by
JOSÉ FELICIANO

GRANDMA GOT RUN OVER BY A REINDEER

TRUMPET

Words and Music by
RANDY BROOKS

THE GREATEST GIFT OF ALL

TRUMPET

Words and Music by
JOHN JARVIS

Moderately slow

GOOD KING WENCESLAS

Words by JOHN M. NEALE
Music from *Piae Cantiones*

GROWN-UP CHRISTMAS LIST

TRUMPET

Words and Music by DAVID FOSTER
and LINDA THOMPSON-JENNER

Moderately slow

HARK! THE HERALD ANGELS SING

Words by CHARLES WESLEY
Music by FELIX MENDELSSOHN-BARTHOLDY

Moderately

HAPPY XMAS
(War Is Over)

TRUMPET

Written by JOHN LENNON
and YOKO ONO

Moderately

To Coda

D.S. al Coda

CODA

HAVE YOURSELF A MERRY LITTLE CHRISTMAS

from MEET ME IN ST. LOUIS

TRUMPET

Words and Music by HUGH MARTIN
and RALPH BLANE

HAPPY HOLIDAY

from the Motion Picture Irving Berlin's HOLIDAY INN

TRUMPET

Words and Music by
IRVING BERLIN

Slowly

HARD CANDY CHRISTMAS

from THE BEST LITTLE WHOREHOUSE IN TEXAS

Words and Music by
CAROL HALL

Moderately

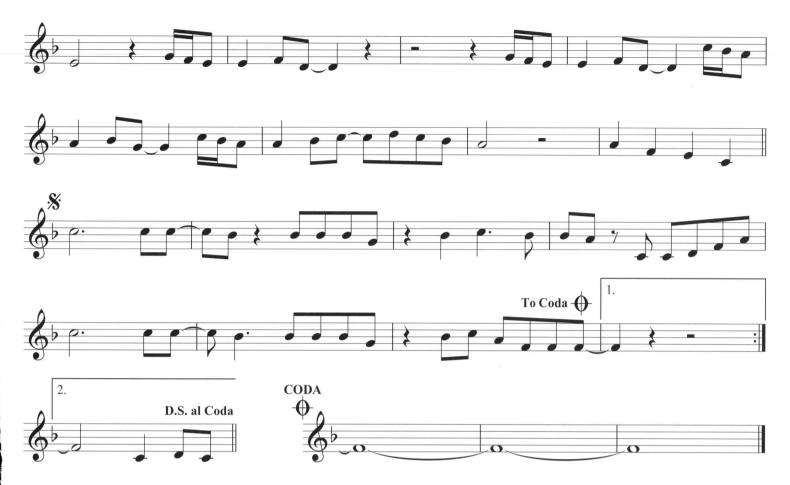

HERE COMES SANTA CLAUS
(Right Down Santa Claus Lane)

Words and Music by GENE AUTRY
and OAKLEY HALDEMAN

TRUMPET

(There's No Place Like)
HOME FOR THE HOLIDAYS

Words and Music by AL STILLMAN
and ROBERT ALLEN

Moderately

I HEARD THE BELLS ON CHRISTMAS DAY

TRUMPET

Words by HENRY WADSWORTH LONGFELLOW
Music by JOHN BAPTISTE CALKIN

A HOLLY JOLLY CHRISTMAS

Music and Lyrics by
JOHNNY MARKS

I WANT A HIPPOPOTAMUS FOR CHRISTMAS
(Hippo the Hero)

TRUMPET

Words and Music by
JOHN ROX

Brightly

I'LL BE HOME FOR CHRISTMAS

Words and Music by KIM GANNON
and WALTER KENT

Slowly

I HEARD THE BELLS ON CHRISTMAS DAY

TRUMPET

Words by HENRY WADSWORTH LONGFELLOW
Adapted by JOHNNY MARKS
Music by JOHNNY MARKS

Moderately

I SAW MOMMY KISSING SANTA CLAUS

Words and Music by
TOMMIE CONNOR

Moderately slow

I SAW THREE SHIPS

TRUMPET

Traditional English Carol

Brightly

I WONDER AS I WANDER

By JOHN JACOB NILES

Slowly

I'VE GOT MY LOVE TO KEEP ME WARM

from the 20th Century Fox Motion Picture ON THE AVENUE

TRUMPET

Words and Music by
IRVING BERLIN

Bright Jump tempo

IT'S BEGINNING TO LOOK LIKE CHRISTMAS

TRUMPET

By MEREDITH WILLSON

IT MUST HAVE BEEN THE MISTLETOE
(Our First Christmas)

TRUMPET

By JUSTIN WILDE
and DOUG KONECKY

IT CAME UPON THE MIDNIGHT CLEAR

Words by EDMUND H. SEARS
Traditional English Melody
Adapted by ARTHUR SULLIVAN

Moderately

JINGLE BELLS

TRUMPET

Words and Music by
J. PIERPONT

Brightly

THE LAST MONTH OF THE YEAR
(What Month Was Jesus Born In?)

Words and Music by VERA HALL
Adapted and Arranged by RUBY PICKENS TARTT
and ALAN LOMAX

Moderately

LET IT SNOW! LET IT SNOW! LET IT SNOW!

Words by SAMMY CAHN
Music by JULE STYNE

JOY TO THE WORLD

TRUMPET

Words by ISAAC WATTS
Music by GEORGE FRIDERIC HANDEL

Brightly

MARY'S LITTLE BOY CHILD

Words and Music by
JESTER HAIRSTON

Slowly and simply

LITTLE SAINT NICK

TRUMPET

Words and Music by BRIAN WILSON
and MIKE LOVE

MARCH OF THE TOYS

from BABES IN TOYLAND

TRUMPET

By VICTOR HERBERT

With spirit

(small note optional)

A MARSHMALLOW WORLD

TRUMPET

Words by CARL SIGMAN
Music by PETER DE ROSE

MARY, DID YOU KNOW?

TRUMPET

Words and Music by MARK LOWRY
and BUDDY GREENE

MERRY CHRISTMAS, DARLING

TRUMPET

Words and Music by RICHARD CARPENTER
and FRANK POOLER

THE MOST WONDERFUL TIME OF THE YEAR

TRUMPET

Words and Music by EDDIE POLA
and GEORGE WYLE

MY FAVORITE THINGS

from THE SOUND OF MUSIC

TRUMPET

Lyrics by OSCAR HAMMERSTEIN II
Music by RICHARD RODGERS

Lively

MELE KALIKIMAKA

TRUMPET

Words and Music by
R. ALEX ANDERSON

Brightly

MISTER SANTA

Words and Music by
PAT BALLARD

Bright

MISTLETOE AND HOLLY

Words and Music by FRANK SINATRA,
DOK STANFORD and HENRY W. SANICOLA

Medium Bounce

O LITTLE TOWN OF BETHLEHEM

TRUMPET

Words by PHILLIPS BROOKS
Music by LEWIS H. REDNER

O HOLY NIGHT

French words by PLACIDE CAPPEAU
English words by JOHN S. DWIGHT
Music by ADOLPHE ADAM

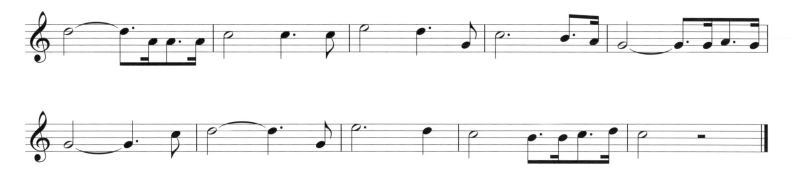

SANTA CLAUS IS COMIN' TO TOWN

Words by HAVEN GILLESPIE
Music by J. FRED COOTS

O CHRISTMAS TREE

TRUMPET

Traditional German Carol

Moderately

O COME, ALL YE FAITHFUL

Music by JOHN FRANCIS WADE

Moderately

PARADE OF THE WOODEN SOLDIERS

TRUMPET

English Lyrics by BALLARD MacDONALD
Music by LEON JESSEL

PRETTY PAPER

TRUMPET

Words and Music by
WILLIE NELSON

ROCKIN' AROUND THE CHRISTMAS TREE

TRUMPET

Music and Lyrics by
JOHNNY MARKS

Moderate Rock

RUDOLPH THE RED-NOSED REINDEER

TRUMPET

Music and Lyrics by
JOHNNY MARKS

SANTA BABY

TRUMPET

By JOAN JAVITS,
PHIL SPRINGER and TONY SPRINGER

SHAKE ME I RATTLE
(Squeeze Me I Cry)

Words and Music by HAL HACKADY
and CHARLES NAYLOR

TRUMPET

SILVER AND GOLD

Music and Lyrics by
JOHNNY MARKS

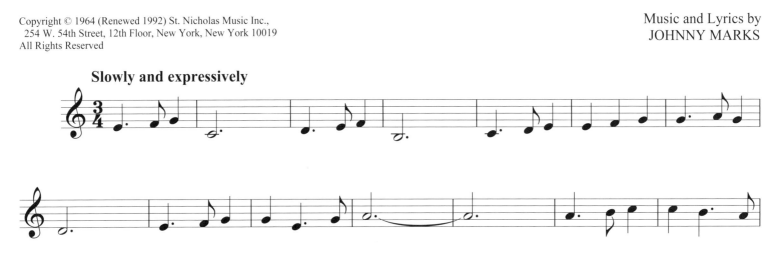

SILVER BELLS
from the Paramount Picture THE LEMON DROP KID

Words and Music by JAY LIVINGSTON
and RAY EVANS

Moderately

THAT'S CHRISTMAS TO ME

TRUMPET

Words and Music by KEVIN OLUSOLA
and SCOTT HOYING

Moderately

SILENT NIGHT

TRUMPET

Words by JOSEPH MOHR
Translated by JOHN F. YOUNG
Music by FRANZ X. GRUBER

SING WE NOW OF CHRISTMAS

Traditional French Carol

SOMEWHERE IN MY MEMORY

from the Twentieth Century Fox Motion Picture HOME ALONE

TRUMPET

Words by LESLIE BRICUSSE
Music by JOHN WILLIAMS

Gently and with simplicity

THE STAR CAROL

Lyric by WIHLA HUTSON
Music by ALFRED BURT

Tenderly, with much expression

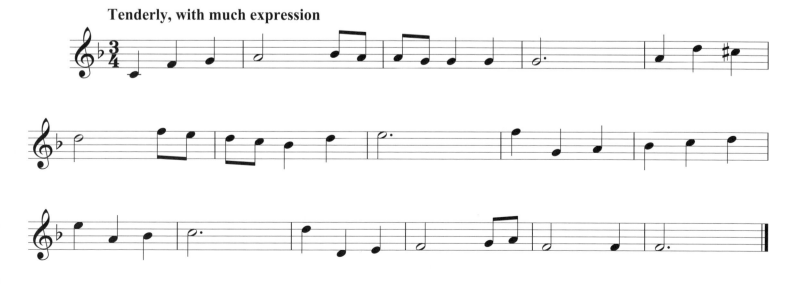

THIS CHRISTMAS

TRUMPET

Words and Music by DONNY HATHAWAY
and NADINE McKINNOR

TOYLAND

from BABES IN TOYLAND

TRUMPET

Words by GLEN MacDONOUGH
Music by VICTOR HERBERT

UP ON THE HOUSETOP

Words and Music by
B.R. HANBY

WE NEED A LITTLE CHRISTMAS

from MAME

TRUMPET

Music and Lyric by
JERRY HERMAN

THE TWELVE DAYS OF CHRISTMAS

TRUMPET

Traditional English Carol

*These bars are played a different number of times for each verse.

WE WISH YOU THE MERRIEST

TRUMPET

Words and Music by
LES BROWN

WE THREE KINGS OF ORIENT ARE

TRUMPET

Words and Music by
JOHN H. HOPKINS, JR.

WE WISH YOU A MERRY CHRISTMAS

Traditional English Folksong

WHAT ARE YOU DOING NEW YEAR'S EVE?

TRUMPET

By FRANK LOESSER

Slowly and sentimentally

WONDERFUL CHRISTMASTIME

TRUMPET

Words and Music by
PAUL McCARTNEY

WHAT CHILD IS THIS?

TRUMPET

Words by WILLIAM C. DIX
16th Century English Melody

Moderately slow

WHITE CHRISTMAS
from the Motion Picture Irving Berlin's HOLIDAY INN

Words and Music by
IRVING BERLIN

Slowly, in 2

YOU'RE ALL I WANT FOR CHRISTMAS

Words and Music by GLEN MOORE
and SEGER ELLIS

Slowly and evenly

THE WONDERFUL WORLD OF CHRISTMAS

TRUMPET

Words by CHARLES TOBIAS
Music by AL FRISCH

101 SONGS

BIG COLLECTIONS OF FAVORITE SONGS ARRANGED FOR SOLO INSTRUMENTALISTS.

101 BROADWAY SONGS

00154199 Flute	$15.99
00154200 Clarinet	$15.99
00154201 Alto Sax	$15.99
00154202 Tenor Sax	$16.99
00154203 Trumpet	$15.99
00154204 Horn	$15.99
00154205 Trombone	$15.99
00154206 Violin	$15.99

00154207 Viola......$15.99
00154208 Cello......$15.99

101 DISNEY SONGS

00244104 Flute	$17.99
00244106 Clarinet	$17.99
00244107 Alto Sax	$17.99
00244108 Tenor Sax	$17.99
00244109 Trumpet	$17.99
00244112 Horn	$17.99
00244120 Trombone	$17.99
00244121 Violin	$17.99

00244125 Viola......$17.99
00244126 Cello......$17.99

101 MOVIE HITS

00158087 Flute	$15.99
00158088 Clarinet	$15.99
00158089 Alto Sax	$15.99
00158090 Tenor Sax	$15.99
00158091 Trumpet	$15.99
00158092 Horn	$15.99
00158093 Trombone	$15.99
00158094 Violin	$15.99

00158095 Viola......$15.99
00158096 Cello......$15.99

101 CHRISTMAS SONGS

00278637 Flute	$15.99
00278638 Clarinet	$15.99
00278639 Alto Sax	$15.99
00278640 Tenor Sax	$15.99
00278641 Trumpet	$15.99
00278642 Horn	$14.99
00278643 Trombone	$15.99
00278644 Violin	$15.99

00278645 Viola......$15.99
00278646 Cello......$15.99

101 HIT SONGS

00194561 Flute	$17.99
00197182 Clarinet	$17.99
00197183 Alto Sax	$17.99
00197184 Tenor Sax	$17.99
00197185 Trumpet	$17.99
00197186 Horn	$17.99
00197187 Trombone	$17.99
00197188 Violin	$17.99

00197189 Viola......$17.99
00197190 Cello......$17.99

101 POPULAR SONGS

00224722 Flute	$17.99
00224723 Clarinet	$17.99
00224724 Alto Sax	$17.99
00224725 Tenor Sax	$17.99
00224726 Trumpet	$17.99
00224727 Horn	$17.99
00224728 Trombone	$17.99
00224729 Violin	$17.99

00224730 Viola......$17.99
00224731 Cello......$17.99

101 CLASSICAL THEMES

00155315 Flute	$15.99
00155317 Clarinet	$15.99
00155318 Alto Sax	$15.99
00155319 Tenor Sax	$15.99
00155320 Trumpet	$15.99
00155321 Horn	$15.99
00155322 Trombone	$15.99
00155323 Violin	$15.99

00155324 Viola......$15.99
00155325 Cello......$15.99

101 JAZZ SONGS

00146363 Flute	$15.99
00146364 Clarinet	$15.99
00146366 Alto Sax	$15.99
00146367 Tenor Sax	$15.99
00146368 Trumpet	$15.99
00146369 Horn	$14.99
00146370 Trombone	$15.99
00146371 Violin	$15.99

00146372 Viola......$15.99
00146373 Cello......$15.99

101 MOST BEAUTIFUL SONGS

00291023 Flute	$16.99
00291041 Clarinet	$16.99
00291042 Alto Sax	$17.99
00291043 Tenor Sax	$17.99
00291044 Trumpet	$16.99
00291045 Horn	$16.99
00291046 Trombone	$16.99
00291047 Violin	$16.99

00291048 Viola......$16.99
00291049 Cello......$17.99

See complete song lists and sample pages at www.halleonard.com

HAL•LEONARD®
www.halleonard.com

Prices, contents and availability subject to change without notice.

HAL•LEONARD INSTRUMENTAL PLAY-ALONG

Your favorite songs are arranged just for solo instrumentalists with this outstanding series. Each book includes great full-accompaniment play-along audio so you can sound just like a pro!

Check out **halleonard.com** for songlists and more titles!

12 Pop Hits
12 songs
00261790	Flute	00261795	Horn
00261791	Clarinet	00261796	Trombone
00261792	Alto Sax	00261797	Violin
00261793	Tenor Sax	00261798	Viola
00261794	Trumpet	00261799	Cello

The Very Best of Bach
15 selections
00225371	Flute	00225376	Horn
00225372	Clarinet	00225377	Trombone
00225373	Alto Sax	00225378	Violin
00225374	Tenor Sax	00225379	Viola
00225375	Trumpet	00225380	Cello

The Beatles
15 songs
00225330	Flute	00225335	Horn
00225331	Clarinet	00225336	Trombone
00225332	Alto Sax	00225337	Violin
00225333	Tenor Sax	00225338	Viola
00225334	Trumpet	00225339	Cello

Chart Hits
12 songs
00146207	Flute	00146212	Horn
00146208	Clarinet	00146213	Trombone
00146209	Alto Sax	00146214	Violin
00146210	Tenor Sax	00146211	Trumpet
00146216	Cello		

Christmas Songs
12 songs
00146855	Flute	00146863	Horn
00146858	Clarinet	00146864	Trombone
00146859	Alto Sax	00146866	Violin
00146860	Tenor Sax	00146867	Viola
00146862	Trumpet	00146868	Cello

Contemporary Broadway
15 songs
00298704	Flute	00298709	Horn
00298705	Clarinet	00298710	Trombone
00298706	Alto Sax	00298711	Violin
00298707	Tenor Sax	00298712	Viola
00298708	Trumpet	00298713	Cello

Disney Movie Hits
12 songs
00841420	Flute	00841424	Horn
00841687	Oboe	00841425	Trombone
00841421	Clarinet	00841426	Violin
00841422	Alto Sax	00841427	Viola
00841686	Tenor Sax	00841428	Cello
00841423	Trumpet		

Prices, contents, and availability subject to change without notice.

Disney characters and artwork ™ & © 2021 Disney

Disney Solos
12 songs
00841404	Flute	00841506	Oboe
00841406	Alto Sax	00841409	Trumpet
00841407	Horn	00841410	Violin
00841411	Viola	00841412	Cello
00841405	Clarinet/Tenor Sax		
00841408	Trombone/Baritone		
00841553	Mallet Percussion		

Dixieland Favorites
15 songs
00268756	Flute	0068759	Trumpet
00268757	Clarinet	00268760	Trombone
00268758	Alto Sax		

Billie Eilish
9 songs
00345648	Flute	00345653	Horn
00345649	Clarinet	00345654	Trombone
00345650	Alto Sax	00345655	Violin
00345651	Tenor Sax	00345656	Viola
00345652	Trumpet	00345657	Cello

Favorite Movie Themes
13 songs
00841166	Flute	00841168	Trumpet
00841167	Clarinet	00841170	Trombone
00841169	Alto Sax	00841296	Violin

Gospel Hymns
15 songs
00194648	Flute	00194654	Trombone
00194649	Clarinet	00194655	Violin
00194650	Alto Sax	00194656	Viola
00194651	Tenor Sax	00194657	Cello
00194652	Trumpet		

Great Classical Themes
15 songs
00292727	Flute	00292733	Horn
00292728	Clarinet	00292735	Trombone
00292729	Alto Sax	00292736	Violin
00292730	Tenor Sax	00292737	Viola
00292732	Trumpet	00292738	Cello

The Greatest Showman
8 songs
00277389	Flute	00277394	Horn
00277390	Clarinet	00277395	Trombone
00277391	Alto Sax	00277396	Violin
00277392	Tenor Sax	00277397	Viola
00277393	Trumpet	00277398	Cello

Irish Favorites
31 songs
00842489	Flute	00842495	Trombone
00842490	Clarinet	00842496	Violin
00842491	Alto Sax	00842497	Viola
00842493	Trumpet	00842498	Cello
00842494	Horn		

Michael Jackson
11 songs
00119495	Flute	00119499	Trumpet
00119496	Clarinet	00119501	Trombone
00119497	Alto Sax	00119503	Violin
00119498	Tenor Sax	00119502	Accomp.

Jazz & Blues
14 songs
00841438	Flute	00841441	Trumpet
00841439	Clarinet	00841443	Trombone
00841440	Alto Sax	00841444	Violin
00841442	Tenor Sax		

Jazz Classics
12 songs
00151812	Flute	00151816	Trumpet
00151813	Clarinet	00151818	Trombone
00151814	Alto Sax	00151819	Violin
00151815	Tenor Sax	00151821	Cello

Les Misérables
13 songs
00842292	Flute	00842297	Horn
00842293	Clarinet	00842298	Trombone
00842294	Alto Sax	00842299	Violin
00842295	Tenor Sax	00842300	Viola
00842296	Trumpet	00842301	Cello

Metallica
12 songs
02501327	Flute	02502454	Horn
02501339	Clarinet	02501329	Trombone
02501332	Alto Sax	02501334	Violin
02501333	Tenor Sax	02501335	Viola
02501330	Trumpet	02501338	Cello

Motown Classics
15 songs
00842572	Flute	00842576	Trumpet
00842573	Clarinet	00842578	Trombone
00842574	Alto Sax	00842579	Violin
00842575	Tenor Sax		

Pirates of the Caribbean
16 songs
00842183	Flute	00842188	Horn
00842184	Clarinet	00842189	Trombone
00842185	Alto Sax	00842190	Violin
00842186	Tenor Sax	00842191	Viola
00842187	Trumpet	00842192	Cello

Queen
17 songs
00285402	Flute	00285407	Horn
00285403	Clarinet	00285408	Trombone
00285404	Alto Sax	00285409	Violin
00285405	Tenor Sax	00285410	Viola
00285406	Trumpet	00285411	Cello

Simple Songs
14 songs
00249081	Flute	00249087	Horn
00249093	Oboe	00249089	Trombone
00249082	Clarinet	00249090	Violin
00249083	Alto Sax	00249091	Viola
00249084	Tenor Sax	00249092	Cello
00249086	Trumpet	00249094	Mallets

Superhero Themes
14 songs
00363195	Flute	00363200	Horn
00363196	Clarinet	00363201	Trombone
00363197	Alto Sax	00363202	Violin
00363198	Tenor Sax	00363203	Viola
00363199	Trumpet	00363204	Cello

Star Wars
16 songs
00350900	Flute	00350907	Horn
00350913	Oboe	00350908	Trombone
00350903	Clarinet	00350909	Violin
00350904	Alto Sax	00350910	Viola
00350905	Tenor Sax	00350911	Cello
00350906	Trumpet	00350914	Mallet

Taylor Swift
15 songs
00842532	Flute	00842537	Horn
00842533	Clarinet	00842538	Trombone
00842534	Alto Sax	00842539	Violin
00842535	Tenor Sax	00842540	Viola
00842536	Trumpet	00842541	Cello

Video Game Music
13 songs
00283877	Flute	00283883	Horn
00283878	Clarinet	00283884	Trombone
00283879	Alto Sax	00283885	Violin
00283880	Tenor Sax	00283886	Viola
00283882	Trumpet	00283887	Cello

Wicked
13 songs
00842236	Flute	00842241	Horn
00842237	Clarinet	00842242	Trombone
00842238	Alto Sax	00842243	Violin
00842239	Tenor Sax	00842244	Viola
00842240	Trumpet	00842245	Cello

HAL•LEONARD®

101 TIPS FROM HAL LEONARD

STUFF ALL THE PROS KNOW AND USE

Ready to take your skills to the next level? These books present valuable how-to insight that musicians of all styles and levels can benefit from. The text, photos, music, diagrams and accompanying audio provide a terrific, easy-to-use resource for a variety of topics.

101 HAMMOND B-3 TIPS
by Brian Charette
Topics include: funky scales and modes; unconventional harmonies; creative chord voicings; cool drawbar settings; ear-grabbing special effects; professional gigging advice; practicing effectively; making good use of the pedals; and much more!
00128918 Book/Online Audio $14.99

101 HARMONICA TIPS
by Steve Cohen
Topics include: techniques, position playing, soloing, accompaniment, the blues, equipment, performance, maintenance, and much more!
00821040 Book/Online Audio $17.99

101 CELLO TIPS—2ND EDITION
by Angela Schmidt
Topics include: bowing techniques, non-classical playing, electric cellos, accessories, gig tips, practicing, recording and much more!
00149094 Book/Online Audio $14.99

101 FLUTE TIPS
by Elaine Schmidt
Topics include: selecting the right flute for you, finding the right teacher, warm-up exercises, practicing effectively, taking good care of your flute, gigging advice, staying and playing healthy, and much more.
00119883 Book/CD Pack..................................$14.99

101 SAXOPHONE TIPS
by Eric Morones
Topics include: techniques; maintenance; equipment; practicing; recording; performance; and much more!
00311082 Book/CD Pack..................................$19.99

101 TRUMPET TIPS
by Scott Barnard
Topics include: techniques, articulation, tone production, soloing, exercises, special effects, equipment, performance, maintenance and much more.
00312082 Book/CD Pack..................................$14.99

101 UPRIGHT BASS TIPS
by Andy McKee
Topics include: right- and left-hand technique, improvising and soloing, practicing, proper care of the instrument, ear training, performance, and much more.
00102009 Book/Online Audio $14.99

101 BASS TIPS
by Gary Willis
Topics include: techniques, improvising and soloing, equipment, practicing, ear training, performance, theory, and much more.
00695542 Book/Online Audio $19.99

101 DRUM TIPS—2ND EDITION
Topics include: grooves, practicing, warming up, tuning, gear, performance, and much more!
00151936 Book/Online Audio $14.99

101 FIVE-STRING BANJO TIPS
by Fred Sokolow
Topics include: techniques, ear training, performance, and much more!
00696647 Book/CD Pack..................................$14.99

101 GUITAR TIPS
by Adam St. James
Topics include: scales, music theory, truss rod adjustments, proper recording studio set-ups, and much more. The book also features snippets of advice from some of the most celebrated guitarists and producers in the music business.
00695737 Book/Online Audio $17.99

101 MANDOLIN TIPS
by Fred Sokolow
Topics include: playing tips, practicing tips, accessories, mandolin history and lore, practical music theory, and much more!
00119493 Book/Online Audio $14.99

101 RECORDING TIPS
by Adam St. James
This book contains recording tips, suggestions, and advice learned firsthand from legendary producers, engineers, and artists. These tricks of the trade will improve anyone's home or pro studio recordings.
00311035 Book/CD Pack..................................$14.95

101 UKULELE TIPS
by Fred Sokolow with Ronny Schiff
Topics include: techniques, improvising and soloing, equipment, practicing, ear training, performance, uke history and lore, and much more!
00696596 Book/Online Audio $15.99

101 VIOLIN TIPS
by Angela Schmidt
Topics include: bowing techniques, non-classical playing, electric violins, accessories, gig tips, practicing, recording, and much more!
00842672 Book/CD Pack..................................$14.99

Prices, contents and availability subject to change without notice.

HAL•LEONARD®

www.halleonard.com